Historical Biographies

MONTEZUMA

Struan Reid

Heinemann Library
Chicago, Illinois

© 2002 Reed Educational & Professional Publishing
Published by Heinemann Library,
an imprint of Reed Educational & Professional Publishing,
Chicago, Illinois

Customer Service 888-454-2279

Visit our website at www.heinemannlibrary.com

Designed by Celia Floyd
Illustrated by Jeff Edwards and Joanna Brooker
Originated by Ambassador Litho Ltd
Printed by Wing King Tong in Hong Kong

06 05 04 03 02
10 9 8 7 6 5 4 3 2 1

Library of Congress Cataloging-in-Publication Data
Reid, Struan.
  Montezuma / Struan Reid.
     p. cm. -- (Historical biographies)
Includes bibliographical references and index.
Summary: Presents an overview of Montezuma's life as well as his
influence on history and the world.
  ISBN 1-58810-566-0 (HC), 1-4034-0101-2 (Pbk.)
  1. Montezuma II, Emperor of Mexico, ca. 1480-1520--Juvenile
literature. 2. Aztecs--Kings and rulers--Biography--Juvenile
literature. 3. Mexico--History--Conquest, 1519-1540--Juvenile
literature. [1. Montezuma II, Emperor of Mexico, ca. 1480-1520. 2.
Kings, queens, rulers, etc. 3. Aztecs--Biography. 4. Indians of
Mexico--Biography. 5. Mexico--History--Conquest, 1519-1540.] I. Title.
II. Series.
  F1230.M6 R45 2002
  972'.02'092--dc21

                                    2001003661

Acknowledgments
The author and publishers are grateful to the following for permission to reproduce copyright material:
Cover photograph: The Art Archive
pp. 5, 6, 9, 14, 29 Bridgeman; pp. 7, 10, 13, 15, 16, 17, 18, 19, 20, 21, 22, 23, 24, 26, 27 The Art
Archive; pp. 8, 11, 25 Corbis; p. 12 AKG; p. 28 South America Pictures.

Special thanks to Rebecca Vickers for her comments in the preparation of this book.

Some words are shown in bold, **like this.** You can find out what they mean
by looking in the glossary.

Many Aztec and Spanish names and terms may be found in the
pronunciation guide.

Contents

Who Was Montezum

Montezuma was a great king and warrior who lived 500 years ago. He ruled over the huge, rich, and powerful Aztec **Empire** in the land now known as Mexico. His territory stretched from the Atlantic to the Pacific Ocean and contained more than 500 towns. The capital city was called Tenochtitlán.

Strangers arrive

In 1519, Montezuma received disturbing news. Some strange-looking men had arrived in his lands and were marching towards Tenochtitlán. These reports seemed to confirm ancient **prophecies** that the Aztec Empire would one day be destroyed by angry and **vengeful** gods. The strangers were not gods at all, but soldiers who had sailed across the Atlantic Ocean from Spain. They had come to conquer the Aztec Empire.

Only 25 years earlier, Europeans had no idea that the continents of North and South America even existed. Then, in 1492, an Italian explorer named Christopher Columbus sailed westward from Spain and arrived in this "New World."

The Aztec Empire

The Aztecs lived in the area of land joining North and South America (now Mexico). Over 3,000 years, this region saw the rise and fall of many great **civilizations**, including the Olmecs, Zapotecs, Maya, and Toltecs. The last of these was the Aztecs. They conquered and ruled a huge empire from about 1420 until 1520.

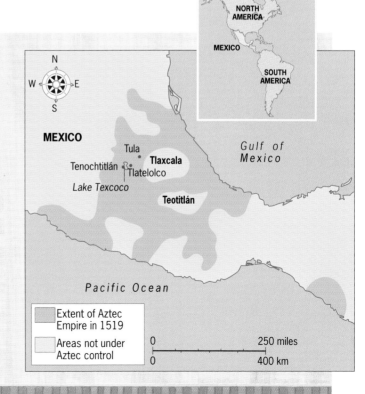

MEXICO

Tula

Tlaxcala

Tenochtitlán

Tlatelolco

Lake Texcoco

Teotitlán

Gulf of Mexico

Pacific Ocean

NORTH AMERICA

MEXICO

SOUTH AMERICA

Extent of Aztec Empire in 1519

Areas not under Aztec control

0   250 miles

0   400 km

The end of the empire

The Aztecs fought to stop the Spaniards from conquering their lands, but within two years, Montezuma was dead. His empire had been destroyed, and most of the Aztec civilization was in ruins. The ancient prophecies had come true, and Montezuma had been the last great ruler of this brilliant empire.

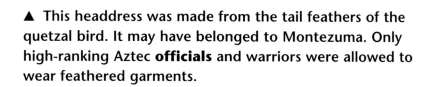

▲ This headdress was made from the tail feathers of the quetzal bird. It may have belonged to Montezuma. Only high-ranking Aztec **officials** and warriors were allowed to wear feathered garments.

Key dates

1325	City of Tenochtitlán **founded**
1430	Growth of Aztec Empire begins
1492	Christopher Columbus sails to the Americas
1502	Montezuma becomes **emperor**
1517	First Spanish expedition reaches Mexico
1520	Death of Montezuma
1521	Tenochtitlán falls to Spanish invaders
1523	Aztec Empire now under Spanish rule; known as New Spain

Montezuma's Early Life

Montezuma was born in about 1466. His parents were members of the Aztec royal family. Another Montezuma, a relative of his father, was **emperor** when baby Montezuma was born. The young boy was brought up as a royal prince.

Montezuma's arrival in the world would have been greeted with celebrations. As soon as Montezuma was born, an **astrologer** would have been sent to the royal palace to help the family choose a name for the prince—a very important decision. Using a calendar of stars, the astrologer also calculated the lucky day on which to name the baby.

▼ Emperor Montezuma is seated on a throne on the left. He is receiving goods such as jaguar skins, woven cloaks, and shields from the cities of his **empire**. This illustration is from a sixteenth-century Spanish account of the Aztecs.

▲ Aztec writing did not use letters and words; instead, they used pictures called glyphs. The dots are numbers. These pictures show the names of four of the days of the month: 5 wind, 6 house, 7 lizard, and 8 snake.

Montezuma's family

Like all Aztec **noblemen**, Montezuma's father had a number of wives. So Montezuma was brought up with many half-brothers and sisters. The family lived in rooms on the top floor of the huge royal palace that lay at the heart of Tenochtitlán.

School days

Montezuma was sent to school at an early age. The school was called a *calmécac*. He was taught with the sons of other noble families. Discipline was very strict, and the students were punished if they did anything wrong. The boys learned reading and writing, astrology, **law**, and mathematics. Their lessons trained them to become priests, **judges**, and army officers. Because he was a member of the royal family, Montezuma was educated as a possible ruler of the Aztec Empire.

Religious training

Religion was extremely important to all Aztecs. Montezuma and his classmates were given a very strict religious training. They were taught to pray and to **fast**. Aztec religion could also be very bloodthirsty—the boys had to perform special **rituals** in which they cut and pierced their own flesh.

Warfare and Games

All Aztec men, from the **emperor** down, were brought up to fight in battle. As he was growing up, Montezuma was taught the skills of warfare. He took part in mock fights with other boys, using wooden swords and shields. By the time he was eighteen, Montezuma had already fought in a number of real battles.

A brave warrior

No Aztec, not even a royal prince, could be honored as a true **nobleman** until he had captured live prisoners in battle. Once Montezuma had done this, he was recognized as a brave and experienced warrior. As a young boy, he had worn his hair long and uncut. Now, as a grown man and warrior, he was allowed to wear it shorter and tied up in a small bunch, called a topknot or crest, on top of his head.

▶ An Aztec soldier who had taken four prisoners in battle could join the special eagle or jaguar troops. This figure is an eagle warrior, wearing armor shaped like an eagle's head and wings.

Playing games

Montezuma and his schoolmates also enjoyed playing games, such as the ball game called *tlachtli.* Only noblemen could play *tlachtli,* because it was part of their religious upbringing, but everyone came to watch and cheer.

Two teams tried to get a small, hard rubber ball through a stone ring mounted high up on a wall. The players were not allowed to touch the ball with their hands—it could be hit only with their hips, elbows, or knees. *Tlachtli* could be dangerous because the ball moved at great speed. Players were often injured and sometimes even killed.

Music and dance

Montezuma was taught to play musical instruments and also learned how to perform special dances for religious ceremonies. Music, song, and dance were enjoyed by everyone and—like almost everything in Aztec life—were closely linked to religion.

▲ This picture shows a group of Aztec musicians. The two men in the middle are playing drums, and the others are playing rattles made from **gourds.**

Aztec Society

The Aztecs had not always lived in Mexico. According to their own **legends**, they had moved there from a land to the north, called Aztlan. For many years, the Aztecs wandered through deserts. Then, in about 1325, they settled on an island in the middle of Lake Texcoco. They called the site Tenochtitlán, meaning "Place of the Fruit of the Cactus." This settlement marked the beginning of the Aztecs' rise to power.

▲ According to legend, the god Huitzilopochtli ordered the Aztecs to settle where they saw an eagle in a cactus, with a serpent in its beak. They spotted this strange sight on an island in Lake Texcoco, where they **founded** Tenochtitlán.

Social classes

The **emperor** was the most important person in Aztec society. Below him were the great nobles called *pipiltin*, who owned land, and *tecuhtli*, who helped him to rule. They were the generals and **judges** who ran the daily life in the cities. Most Aztec people were the *macehualtin*, or common people. The lowest group of all were the slaves. Some were prisoners of war, and others were Aztecs who had fallen on hard times.

The Aztec gods

The Aztecs worshiped many different gods. As well as being the ruler of his people, an emperor was also the Aztec high priest, the most important religious leader. It was important that the gods were kept happy, and the Aztecs believed that the best way of doing this was to give them human blood. Aztec priests **sacrificed** thousands of men, women, and children to the war and sun god, Huitzilopochtli. He was given a daily diet of human hearts to make sure that he would rise the next morning. When Montezuma became emperor, he would have had to perform some of these sacrifices.

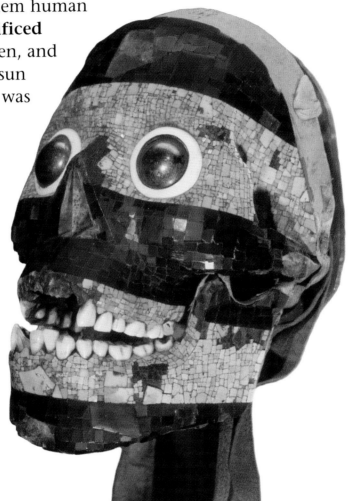

▶ This skull is decorated with turquoise mosaics. It represents Tezcatlipoca, the Aztec god of fate.

Two calendars

The Aztecs had two calendars. The first was called *xiuhpohualli,* "the counting of the years." It was used to figure out the seasons. This was very important for planning the farming year. The second calendar was called the *tonalpohualli,* "the counting of the days." It was used by priests and **astrologers** to predict the future.

Montezuma
the Emperor

At the age of about twenty, Montezuma would have married. He was allowed to marry several wives. He was chosen **emperor** in 1502, at the age of about 36. Montezuma succeeded his great-uncle, Ahuitzotl. He was chosen from all the royal princes by a council of nobles, priests, and military leaders, because they believed that he had the best qualities to be emperor.

Montezuma's coronation

After his election, Montezuma had to spend four days alone in the temple of the sun god, Huitzilopochtli. There, he **fasted** and **meditated** in preparation for the difficult work he had been chosen to do. At Montezuma's **coronation** ceremony, many religious **sacrifices** were made in the temples, followed by a great feast in the royal palace. The leaders of the peoples ruled by the Aztecs were ordered to attend the coronation to show their respect for the new emperor.

◄ All Aztec soldiers carried a shield for protection, but only high-ranking warriors were allowed to have feathered shields. This one was given to Hernán Cortés by Montezuma. It is decorated with a picture of a coyote, the name symbol of emperor Ahuitzotl.

Treated like a god

Montezuma usually appeared in public only at religious ceremonies. When he did, his **noblemen** carried him in a special golden chair, called a litter. He wore beautiful clothes, gold jewelry, and a feathered headdress. No one was allowed to look him directly in the face. So people near him had to bow down and keep their eyes looking at the ground. When Montezuma stepped down from his litter, the floor where he walked was swept. The nobles took off their cloaks and spread them out before him so that his feet never touched the ground.

▲ The Aztecs made jewelry from gold and precious stones such as turquoise and jade. This turquoise ornament, in the shape of a snake, might have been worn on the chest of a priest.

Warlord

Montezuma was chosen to be emperor because of his bravery in battle. After his coronation, he had to prove that he was a good leader by capturing live prisoners to be sacrificed to the gods. Montezuma was away from home fighting for most of the first fifteen years of his reign.

Family Life

When Montezuma was in Tenochtitlán, he lived in the royal palace at the heart of the city. The palace was so huge that one Spanish visitor later wrote: "I walked until I was tired, and never saw the whole of it." It contained hundreds of rooms on two floors. Outside, the palace was surrounded by gardens with ponds and fountains. It even had a large zoo where Montezuma kept wild and exotic animals and birds.

At home with the family

Montezuma and his wives and children lived on the top floor of the palace. There were separate women's quarters, where his wives and daughters spent much of their time spinning, weaving, and making beautiful embroideries. Montezuma always looked very splendid when he appeared in public. At home with his family, however, he lived a very simple life, and his private rooms were plainly decorated.

◀ One of Montezuma's attendants dresses the **emperor** in a **ceremonial** robe and headdress for a public appearance.

Inic v. parrapho ipan mioa imzquitla mantli minechichioaya milatoque ioa incioapipiltm.

▲ All Aztec men wore a **loincloth** and a cloak. This person is a **nobleman,** and his clothes are embroidered and decorated with feathers to show his wealth. The woman wears a loose, decorated blouse over an embroidered skirt.

A room for every occasion

The palace was not just Montezuma's home. He also used it to entertain his nobles, see his advisers, and meet **governors** from the different parts of his **empire.** As many as 600 people would visit him at the palace every day. There were special guest rooms where visiting **ambassadors** could stay. Most of the rooms on the ground floor were used for special occasions—one of them was so big that it could seat 3,000 people. Many of the walls of these official rooms were covered with beautiful paintings, stone and wood carvings, and panels of solid gold.

Palace staff

With so many people visiting every day, thousands of servants were needed to run the palace. There were special rooms for builders and cleaners, for Montezuma's bodyguards, and for the royal servants and slaves. There were huge kitchens where the food for the royal feasts was cooked, and storerooms where all the supplies were kept.

Montezuma's Empire

Montezuma ruled his **empire** with the help of his **noblemen**, army leaders, **judges**, and city leaders. Many of the important positions in the government were held by his relatives. The most important person after Montezuma was his chief adviser. This person was always a man, but was known as the *cihuacoatl,* meaning "snake woman." He was the chief judge, and was in charge of thousands of government **officials.** He also supervised the election of a new **emperor.**

One of the biggest cities in the world

Montezuma's capital city of Tenochtitlán had a population of at least 80,000 people, perhaps even as many as 300,000. This was more than many European cities at that time. It was a beautiful city, full of stone and wooden buildings; clean, wide streets; and many **canals.** In the fields outside the city, the people grew crops of maize, peppers, and cotton.

▼ This plan of Montezuma's capital city, Tenochtitlán, was drawn by the Spaniards. It shows the city on an island in the lake, along with the causeways that linked it to the mainland.

Paying tribute

There were so many people living in the city that they could not possibly grow all the things they needed themselves. The Aztecs had to rely on extra supplies from other parts of their empire.

Every few months, lists of the things needed by the people of Tenochtitlán were sent out to the other **city-states** in the empire. Goods like **grain**, fruit and vegetables, cloth, weapons, and feather headdresses were collected and taken to Tenochtitlán. The items collected were known as **tribute.** These demands for tribute made the Aztecs very unpopular with the people living within their empire.

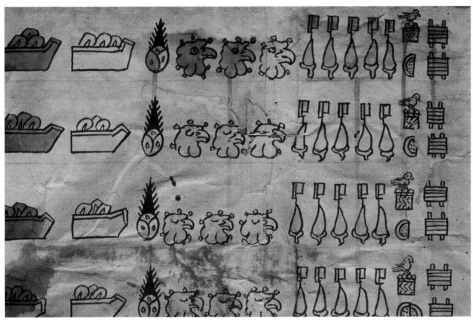

▲ The Aztecs used tribute lists like this one to show what goods a town had to pay. The symbols above the goods show how many were needed. The tree symbol means 400, and the flag means 20.

Picking fights

The other cities in the empire could refuse to pay tribute, but they would be attacked by the Aztecs if they dared to refuse. The Aztecs were almost always fighting with their neighbors. These wars supplied the Aztecs with the great number of prisoners they needed for their human **sacrifices** to the gods.

Warnings from the Gods

      To the Aztec people, Montezuma seemed to be the most powerful ruler in the world. He was a brave warrior and brilliant leader. Riches poured into Tenochtitlán from every part of the **empire**. Montezuma was treated as if he were a god. However, in 1518, when he was at the peak of his power, the lives of the Aztecs would change forever.

Strange omens

Strange things had been happening that disturbed the **emperor.** For several years, Montezuma and his advisers had received **omens** that something terrible was going to happpen. A **comet** was seen blazing in a streak of flames across the skies. Temples were struck by bolts of lightning and burst into flames. Tenochtitlán was hit by sudden floods. Some said they had seen the water in Lake

The legend of Quetzalcoatl

At this time, Montezuma was probably reminded of the **legend** of Quetzalcoatl, a god who long ago had been driven out of the Aztec lands and had sailed away eastward across the seas. One day, it was said, he would come back to destroy the Aztec Empire and take the land for himself.

▶ Quetzalcoatl, the Aztec god of creation, could take many forms. He was often shown as a snake with a green feathered tail. This turquoise mask shows him in his human shape.

▲ This picture shows Montezuma standing on the roof of his palace, watching a comet in the sky. Aztec **astrologers** took this comet as a sign of bad things to come.

Texcoco boil, while others said that in the middle of the night they had heard the voice of a woman, telling them to run away from the city.

A look into the future?

One of the strangest of all these stories concerned some fishermen, who were said to have caught an extraordinary gray bird on the shores of Lake Texcoco. It had a mirror on its head and looked so odd that the fishermen brought it to the emperor. When Montezuma looked into the mirror, he saw warriors, riding on strange-looking beasts, who had come to destroy his empire.

19

Strangers on the Coast

One day, towards the end of 1519, messengers arrived in Tenochtitlán, bringing Montezuma worrying news. They reported that a small army of strange-looking men had been seen on the coast. These men had pale skin and beards. They had arrived in huge craft, as big as mountains, and were riding on four-legged monsters. Montezuma had spies working for him all over the **empire.** They watched the strangers closely and every day sent back reports to their master.

▲ This picture shows the arrival of the first Spanish ship on the coast of Mexico. An Aztec is hiding in the tree, watching and waiting to report what he has seen.

Men or gods?

Montezuma was probably in a panic. These reports would have confirmed his greatest fear—the god Quetzalcoatl had returned at last to reclaim his kingdom. How was Montezuma supposed to deal with these unwelcome visitors? If they really were gods, then they would have to be welcomed and treated with respect. If they were soldiers who had come to attack his empire, he would have to fight them.

Adventurers from Spain

In fact, the visitors were a band of about 500 Spanish soldiers. The "craft as big as mountains" that they traveled in were ships, and the "four-legged monsters" they rode were horses. They were led by a soldier and **adventurer** named Hernán Cortés, and had come in search of a land full of gold and treasure.

The very day that Cortés and his men arrived in Mexico was also the birthday of Quetzalcoatl. This was exactly the time when Aztec **legends** claimed that the god would return to destroy their empire.

▶ This is Hernán Cortés, leader of the Spanish soldiers. He is wearing armor, but the Aztecs thought it was a metal skin.

Hernán Cortés (1485–1547)

Hernán Cortés had read stories of the great riches to be found in the Americas, and came to Mexico in search of gold. In 1519, he set out to capture the Aztec Empire and claim it for Spain. From 1523–1526, Cortés ruled as **governor** of "New Spain," as the empire became known. He eventually fell from power and died forgotten in southern Spain.

Montezuma Panics

As Montezuma heard more about the visitors to his lands, he probably grew very frightened. He learned that the strangers had asked questions about him and wanted to meet him. But at first Montezuma did nothing.

Gifts of gold

Then Montezuma decided to send gifts to the strangers. One of the gifts was a huge dish made of solid gold. This present may have been intended as a warning to the visitors that Montezuma was the richest and most powerful ruler in the world, so they had better leave. However, these rich gifts did not warn off the Spaniards, but only made them want more gold.

Montezuma probably hoped that these unwelcome visitors would just go away. But in August 1519, they started to march toward the heart of Montezuma's **empire**. Along the way, they recruited warriors from enemies of the Aztecs.

▼ Montezuma, seated on his throne, is instructing the messengers he is sending to the Spaniards.

The army arrives

Montezuma heard about the growing army that was heading closer. He sent more messengers to try and persuade them to go away. He set **ambushes** and traps, but nothing could stop them. Finally, the Spaniards and their followers reached the shores of Lake Texcoco and saw the great city of Tenochtitlán for the first time. Montezuma was still unsure whether these strangers were gods or humans. He was about to find out.

▲ This painting shows the princes of Tlaxcala, a place the Aztecs had not conquered. Here, they are agreeing to help the Spaniards fight against the Aztecs.

Doña Marina

One of the people traveling with the Spaniards was a woman named Malintzin. She came from a tribe that hated the Aztecs. The Spaniards renamed her Doña Marina. She learned to speak Spanish and acted as **interpreter** for Cortés. It was through her help that the Spaniards were able to recruit so many extra warriors.

The Death of Montezuma

The Spaniards began to walk along one of the causeways that led across the lake to Tenochtitlán. Suddenly, coming towards them, they saw a wonderful sight. Montezuma himself had come to greet them. He was carried in his golden litter, and dressed in his most splendid **ceremonial** robes. The Spaniards were presented with gifts, and Montezuma gave them a speech of welcome.

▲ This picture shows Montezuma and Cortés in the royal palace at Tenochtitlán, with Doña Marina as their **interpreter**.

Under arrest

Then they were escorted into the city and housed in one of the smaller royal palaces. The Spaniards were to be the guests of the **emperor**. Cortés knew that it was only the **goodwill** of Montezuma that prevented them from being killed. Less than two weeks after they arrived, the Spaniards suddenly arrested and imprisoned Montezuma.

Killed by his own people?

Six months later, fighting broke out between the Aztecs and Spaniards. Cortés ordered Montezuma to speak to his people and calm the situation. The Aztecs had lost all respect for Montezuma. When he appeared on the palace balcony, the angry crowds threw stones at him. It is said that one large stone struck him on the head, and Montezuma fell to the floor. He was carried back into the palace, where he died soon afterward.

The Spaniards claimed that Montezuma had died from his head wound, but the Aztecs said that he must have been strangled by the Spaniards. Montezuma had once been treated like a god, but at the end of his life, he was hated and despised by his own people.

▶ This gold pendant was made by highly skilled Mixtec craftsmen, who supplied jewelry to the Aztecs.

Hidden treasure

The Spaniards discovered a secret room in the palace where they were staying. When they broke through the wall, they found that the room was piled high with Montezuma's gold, silver, and jewels. These things were what they had really sailed all the way from Spain to find.

The End of the Aztec Empire

The Aztecs were now determined to kill the Spaniards who had come to conquer them. Cortés and his men had to leave Tenochtitlán as soon as they could. One night, they tried to escape from the city. As they were creeping away, they were attacked by a huge Aztec army that was waiting for them. Many of the Spaniards were killed or dragged away to be **sacrificed** to the gods.

Tenochtitlán under siege

Cortés and some of his men managed to escape. He formed a huge new army from the Aztecs' enemies and marched back to Tenochtitlán. They surrounded the city, cutting off the food and water supplies, so the people inside began to starve. For several long months, the Aztecs fought back. Another **emperor**, a nephew of Montezuma's named Cuauhtémoc, had been elected. He swore to his people that he would defend the **empire** to the death.

◀ This picture shows a scene from *La Noche Triste*. As Cortés and his men try to escape, they are attacked by Aztec soldiers, some of them dressed as eagle and jaguar warriors.

La Noche Triste

The night Cortés and his soldiers tried to escape from Tenochtitlán is known as *La Noche Triste,* meaning "the sad night" in Spanish. More than two-thirds of the Spaniards were killed on the causeway leading across Lake Texcoco. Many of them drowned, weighed down by the golden treasures they had stolen from Montezuma's palace.

The Aztecs surrender

Finally, the Spaniards and their supporters were able to break into the city. There was bitter fighting in the streets, but the Aztecs' weapons were no match for the guns and steel swords of the Spaniards. One day, the new emperor, Cuauhtémoc, was caught trying to escape from the city. When news of his **treachery** reached the ears of the brave Aztec warriors, they surrendered. Tenochtitlán was finally captured by the Spaniards in August 1521. The once magnificent city now lay in ruins.

▼ In the battle for Tenochtitlán, Spanish and Aztec soldiers are fighting on one of the causeways. The bodies of dead soldiers are floating in the water nearby.

After Montezuma

When Tenochtitlán fell to the Spaniards, they swept through the ruined city, killing thousands of Aztecs. The remaining Aztec temples were destroyed, and the people were forbidden to practice their old religion.

Slavery and disease

Hernán Cortés was appointed **governor** of New Spain, as Montezuma's old **empire** was now called. Christian churches were built on the ruins of many Aztec temples. Thousands of Aztecs and the other peoples who lived in Mexico died from warfare and slavery. Many more were killed by smallpox and other **diseases** that the Spaniards had carried with them from Europe. The Aztecs had no resistance to these diseases. Just 80 years after the death of Montezuma, three-quarters of his people had died out. Three hundred years passed before Mexico won back its **independence** from Spain.

▼ The Spaniards built a huge cathedral on the site of the Great Temple that stood next to Montezuma's palace. These ruins are all that is left of the Great Temple today.

Legacy of the Aztecs

The people of Mexico today have inherited many Aztec and Spanish traditions. The descendants of the Aztecs are now known as the Nahua. The Aztec language is still spoken in parts of Mexico, and some of the old Aztec religious ceremonies are still celebrated there as part of the Christian religion. Montezuma's family lived on for many generations. His oldest son was named "Count of Montezuma" by the king of Spain, and some of his descendants eventually became governors of New Spain.

How do we know?

We know about Montezuma and the Aztecs from the **records** they kept and from the accounts written by their Spanish conquerors. The Aztecs recorded their history and details of their daily lives, **laws**, gods, and **customs** in books now called codices. Many of these were destroyed by the Spaniards, but a few have survived.

▲ Montezuma, **emperor** of the Aztecs, is shown being carried in his golden litter. The Spanish artist, Miguel Gonzalez, has shown Montezuma wearing a European-style crown and clothes.

Most of the Aztec buildings and the objects inside them were also destroyed. The few objects that survived, such as pottery, embroidery, and sculptures provide us with valuable information about the Aztecs.

Glossary

adventurer person who looks for adventure, and especially who looks for success or money through daring deeds

ambassador representative sent by the government of a ruling group or country to visit other rulers or countries

ambush sudden attack from a hidden position

astrologer person who tries to predict the future by observing the positions of the stars and planets

canal artificial waterway built to water crops or to transport goods

ceremonial relating to a formal rite

city-state separate state limited to the area within the city walls and the land surrounding it

civilization highly developed, organized society

comet huge ball of dust, ice, and gas that travels around the sun, often followed by a tail of gas

coronation ceremony for crowning a monarch

custom practice or habit, or the usual way of doing something

disease illness

emperor ruler of an empire

empire large land or group of lands ruled by one person or government

fast to stop eating all or certain foods, especially for religious reasons

found to start something, such as a city or school

goodwill friendly feelings

gourd hard-skinned fruit that can be hollowed out and used as a container

governor person who rules a city or land for another person, such as a king

grain seeds from grasses that can be eaten, such as corn

independence freedom from control

interpreter person who translates from one language to another

judge official who presides over a court of law and passes judgment

law rule or set of rules to control people's behavior

legend ancient story

loincloth piece of cloth worn hanging down from the waist in front and back

meditate to think deeply about something, especially a religious or spiritual matter

nobleman man of the highest rank in Aztec society (after the emperor)

official person who holds a position in a government or some other organization

omen event regarded as a sign of future happiness or disaster

prophecy message foretelling future events

record account, especially in writing, that keeps knowledge or information safe

ritual well-used form of a religious or traditional ceremony

sacrifice to kill a person or animal as an offering to the gods

treachery betrayal of someone's trust

tribute gift given to a ruler by people, often paid as a kind of tax

vengeful wanting to take revenge

Time Line

About 1466	Birth of Montezuma II
About 1486–1502	Rule of the Aztec **emperor** Ahuitzotl
1492–93	Christopher Columbus reaches the Bahamas and West Indies
1500	Aztec **Empire** reaches its biggest size under emperor Ahuitzotl
1502	Montezuma II becomes emperor of the Aztecs after the death of his great-uncle Ahuitzotl
1517	The Spanish first reach the coast of Mexico
1519	Hernán Cortés and his Spanish soldiers reach Tenochtitlán
1520	Death of Montezuma
1521	Collapse of the Aztec Empire
1523	All of Aztec Empire ruled by Spain

Pronunciation Guide

Word	You say
Ahuitzotl	ah-weet-SOT-l
codices	KO-di-seez
Cuauhtémoc	kwow-TAY-mock
Doña	DOHN-yah
glyph	glif
Hernán Cortés	air-NAHN kor-TEZ
Huitzilopochtli	weet-zeel-oh-POCH-tlee
La Noche Triste	lah NO-chay TREESE-tay
macehualtin	MAH-say-WAHL-teen
Quetzalcoatl	ket-sahl-ko-AH-tl
Tenochtitlán	teh-noch-teet-LAHN
Teotitlán	TAY-oh-teet-LAHN
tlachtli	TLAHCH-tlee
Tlatelolco	TLAHT-el-OHL-ko
Tlaxcala	Tlahs-KAHL-ah

More Books to Read

Ganeri, Anita. *The Aztecs*. Austin, Tex.: Raintree Steck-Vaughn, 2000.

Kimmel, Eric A. *Montezuma & the Fall of the Aztecs*. New York: Holiday House, Incorporated, 2000.

Steele, Philip. *The Aztec News*. Milwaukee, Wis.: Gareth Stevens, 2001.

Index